Muffins for tea

Muffins for tea

(an evacuee's story)

by

Doris Corti

First published in 2019
by Hillfold Publishing

ISBN   978-0-244-52243-8

Printed and bound by Lulu.com

ACKNOWLEDGEMENTS

Some of the poems in this book have appeared in the collections

Kingfisher & other things   Scriptora
Rituals and Reminders   The Estuary Press
The Tumbling Sky   Headland

Summer's End was published by Stride in *The Unsaid Goodnight* and by Macmillan Children's Books in *I remember, I remember*

Waiting to be Met (An Evacuee, 1940) was published by Cassell in *Marigolds Grow Wild on Platforms* and by Hodder Children's Books in *Blood and Roses*

NON-FICTION BOOKS BY DORIS CORTI

Writing Poetry   Thomas & Lochar
Successful Grandparenting   How To Books Ltd
Lavender Blues   Poetry Monthly Press

AUTHOR'S NOTE

Thanks to all who helped me in the writing and publishing of this book.

Especial thanks to my two sons Jeff Stump editor/adviser and Mick Stump cover design, also to Alison and Malcolm Chisholm for their invaluable help all through the production of this book. Without their help and guidance I could not have managed.

Doris Corti

A versatile freelance writer and poet, Doris Corti writes under her maiden name. A Vice President of The Society of Women Writers & Journalists, her work has appeared in many poetry magazines and anthologies. She writes a regular column for 'Writing Magazine', wrote the Home Study Course for 'Writers' News' and currently leads a U3A group for writing poetry. Now a nonagenarian, she has written a mini memoir covering the decade 1939-1949 including the time when she was an evacuee during World War two.

CONTENTS

FOREWORD

I have always known Doris Corti as a fine and skilled poet whose measured lines and wonderful sense of rhythm are perfectly crafted. So it was magical to read her prose account of growing up during the wartime years, moving from childhood through adolescence to adulthood. The poetry is still there in the fine use of language and imagery.

The emotional journey that all children must make is bordered, here, by the presence of air raids and Hitler's 'terror weapons'. Doris Corti never falls into the trap of waxing lyrical about bombs and bayonets - a skilful writer, she does not ignore the perils, everything is well handled.

A fascinating monograph, it is the growing process during a time of war and disaster that is important. I don't think I have read a better account of life in those terrible but, as she reminds us in her finely crafted prose, still fascinating years.

There are several wonderful little cameos, building the Anderson shelter for one, and the regular arrival of the Muffin man. The image of Doris running with her 'silver money' to buy six muffins from the man who stood in the lamplight to sell his wares will stay with me for a long time - it seems to symbolise a world that was forever changing.

The process of evacuation is also well handled. 'Years after I was to think of it as something resembling a cattle market' Doris says of the selection process evacuees endured once they had reached their destination.

A return to London, first job and meeting with the 'strong, brave young man' who was to become her husband is well told, without the sentimentality that haunts all remembrances pieces. Avoiding sentimentality but retaining the ability to clutch at the heart is the gift of all poets. Doris Corti has it in spades!

The added bonus of a poem at the beginning of each chapter fits well with the prose, reminding us that she is a writer of real skill and ability in whichever genre she chooses to work. A beautiful book to read, treasure and enjoy. I cannot recommend it enough.

Phil Carradice, poet, novelist and historian. He has published over 80 books and regularly broadcasts on TV and radio. He presents the BBC Wales history programme 'The Past Master.'

For my family

Someone said that God gave us memory so that we might
have roses in December.

J.M.Barrie (1860-1937).

Chapter One - Childhood

Summer's End

I remember the long days,
long, hot evermore days
and the gathering of children
after school, gangland games
and trains under planked bridges
that sighed smoke,
as we peered through cracks.

The summer of gold days,
edge-of-the-world heat-high days;
railings that fenced our square
and one straggling rose,
that grew red in the dead of the dust,

and the rabbit, pushing his nose
through the cage on top of the shed,
long Sunday mornings with the papers read –
in the kitchen – windows steaming,
myself dreaming, kneeling to look out
at summer staying the same,
and boys who were passing calling my name.

The end of the summer,
evacuee time, with the long line of us
weaving down to the train, and parents who came
and cried, and summer's end
was a world that died.

The changes didn't seem noticeable at first; well not to me. I expect the adults were more aware. In 1939 I was eleven with all the days of my childhood filled with home, school, friends and games.

Of course, that first siren as soon as war was declared was strange. It seemed to echo throughout our small terraced house, and to this day when I hear the siren on an ambulance or police car I grow tense. When this first warning went I was recovering in my bed from rheumatic fever. Dad carried me downstairs and all of us managed to crouch in the cupboard under the stairs, where we hoped we would be protected from any bombs. We came out relieved when we heard the reassuring sound of the all clear. It had been a practice warning.

When I was well again we had the fitting of the gasmasks. I did find things beginning to get a little strange by then, and those fittings were surreal. The smell of rubber was very strong as all the gasmasks were unpacked and given out to lots of people who were crowding into school or church halls, with younger children crying. My brother was already a sailor in the Royal Navy, and my Dad, determined to do his bit for the war effort became an air-raid warden. Meanwhile Mum, who was always Mum, kept the pots boiling. Regular as clockwork she cleaned our house, and well, she was always just there; and me? I became an evacuee. That's farther on in the story, so I'll go back a bit, before that first air-raid warning.

I grew up hearing talk about the depression, but life, at least as far as I was concerned in my early years, was a happy one. We were not a wealthy family and like many others in my East End of London neighbourhood my parents worked; Dad as painter and decorator, and glazier as he was proud to add, having done his apprenticeship. Mum was a trained cook and was not too proud to take on that, as well as housework, for some of the more wealthy families in our area. I ran into school quite happily when the teacher rang the old hand bell.

Although not clever, I enjoyed the time there with friends, and had enough pence in my pocket to buy a few sweets in the corner shop on the way home.

Saturday late afternoons a different bell was heard in our street. The Muffin man, with a tray on his head full of our Saturday treat, rang another hand bell and called or sang out 'the Muffin man'. He stood under lamplight near our house and I was given silver money to run and buy 6 muffins. Once home we toasted them by the glowing coal fire, smothered them in butter and sometimes honey. They were good times and we were a loving family.

Soon my days were changing. We had an air-raid shelter delivered in metal parts. If you had a garden, which we did, you could dig a hole out of the soil 6ft deep, and this shed-like thing was 6ft high and 4ft 5 wide and 6ft 5 long. It had to be put 4ft in the ground and have 15 inches of soil on top of its roof. This took quite a bit of digging and building, but all the neighbours helped each other. Steps led down into the shelter and it was supplied with bunk beds. We had them set up one side of the shelter and Mum and Dad had a deck chair each on the other side. Two buckets were also supplied – one for water, and you can guess what the other was for.

Dad told me they were called Anderson shelters. Some folk chose to have a shelter indoors, under some furniture I think, and this was called a Morrison shelter.

That, and the fact that they came and took away our lovely green railings that edged our tiny front garden area, seemed very strange. 'They will bring them back again won't they?' I asked Dad, and wondered why he smiled. By now I was aware that we were entering into some time that was not just to change my little area of life, but the whole world.

Looking back I realise what a momentous decision my parents had to make about me becoming an evacuee. Because of my recovery time following rheumatic fever I did not go with the first lot of school children. I would go with the next evacuation. Mum and Dad carefully explained to me that as we we lived in an area of London that was near the docks we were bound to have bombs dropped on us. Worried for my safety, they thought it best for me to travel with the next lot of evacuees, most of them my friends, to the safety of some distant and as yet unknown place. I understood, and always knew, that they did this because they loved me. I found nothing at that time too disturbing. I didn't really know much about bombs, and the only thing I knew about war was when I had seen badly disabled and blind men begging in our streets. They had been in another war, I was told. It seemed a grim end for them, but in those lovely, long ago childhood days my mind didn't linger long about what had happened all those years ago.

The events in my own life were, it seemed, beginning to affect me. I had sat the 'scholarship' or 11 plus by then, so it was agreed that I would be leaving as an evacuee when arrangements had been made. Schools were open at the start of the war, or rather, I don't think all of them were but mine was. Certainly my familiar pattern didn't seem too disrupted and I could still attend my regular guide meeting. The only hazard I found doing that was that when I left the meeting it was getting dark and made darker by the fact that the blackout had come into force immediately war was declared. No lamps were lit in any street and no lights shone out from windows on houses, as they were covered with black blinds or thick curtains. At eleven I declared that I was quite old enough to come home alone. Respecting my wishes, Dad got me a special torch with a yellow bulb and with its face partially obscured. I did acquiesce, however, and agreed to carry my gasmask in the correct case and not one of those fancy design ones that I'd bought in the Saturday market. He explained the gasmask might be pulled out of shape by this more fashionable design. I agreed, because I knew that all they did was out of consideration and love for me.

Coming out from guides with a few friends, then running home after I left each of them in the roads where they lived, I felt no fear. Although, have you ever come through heavy rain in the dark? It's a bit hazardous, but I knew once home with Mum and Dad, the kettle boiling on top of the hob and bright lights behind our thick curtains, that I'd be safe. I hardly gave any thought to the coming war. Oh. I thought of it of course, when I heard the grown ups talking about it, but it seemed unreal and far away.

When the day came for me to leave home I promised my parents that I would be brave and good. Mum took me to the school where I met the other children who were travelling with me. I said my goodbyes there, more nervous than excited. We didn't know where we were going, parents had merely been told that we were going far west. Mum waved me goodbye. She didn't cry like some of the Mums, and because of her bravery I managed to hold back my tears, although some of the younger children did cry.

It was noisy at the big London station, porters and guards shouting and whistles blowing. Some of the younger children were frightened. I had been on a big station like this before when we went to visit my aunt who lived in Brighton. Somehow in the midst of all the noise and what seemed like confusion, the teachers and guards got us settled in our carriages. I had sandwiches – Mum wouldn't let me go without food – we had water to drink and mostly I settled down to read a comic. The trains had corridors with big windows, but once in my seat I stayed unless I had to go to the toilet which was at the end of the corridor. Sometimes the teachers asked me to comfort one of the younger children who was frightened and crying.

Well, Mum and Dad had been given the right information. After a very long journey, it was the west of the country we arrived at – Cornwall, where we were taken to a big hall. Perhaps it was a school hall or a church room, I don't

15

know. I was tired, and did cry then. I was hungry and bewildered. Perhaps I thought it was all a dream, but it wasn't. We had to go through a selection by all sorts of people coming to decide who they would take home as their chosen evacuee. No one wanted my friend Doreen and me, as we wanted to stay together.

So many people looked us over and I heard loud voices all round me saying 'I'll have that one', as they chose a child from amongst the throng of children. Years after I was to think of it as something resembling a cattle market. After many hours a friendly lady and her husband came over to where Doreen and I sat at a school desk, and asked our names and said if we liked we could go to their house where we would have something to eat and drink and stay there.

This place we had arrived at was called St. Ives. That night we slept in twin beds in a cosy bedroom. I woke up to the sound of seagulls, something that would become familiar to me.

I became fascinated by that place. How different it was from my home in West Ham. I remember all those people in Cornwall and that glorious summer. Doreen my friend was happy too, and we wrote home continually saying how everyone made a fuss of us and how happy we were. We felt it was our second home. All these lovely new things crowded in on me, and although I missed Mum and Dad a lot I enjoyed St.Ives.

We adopted Mr. and Mrs. Clare who had kindly taken us into their home, and we and called them Uncle and Aunt. They had three children, a son in the R.A.F. – we were given his bedroom – also two daughters, one eighteen, who was in a reserved occupation in the main post office, and another girl three years older than me. We all got on well and the eldest girl, Rita, who intended to be a school teacher after the war, encouraged my love of reading and writing, particularly encouraging my love of poetry. I often sat and read from her book, *The Golden Treasury of Verse*, and found it a great comfort when sometimes I felt a bit homesick, even though I loved the big beaches and being woken each morning to the sound of gulls over the rooftops.

I wrote home a lot and told them I was happy and received letters from Mum and Dad who sounded cheerful. How they must have looked out for my letters. They had been right to send me away, I missed the Battle of Britain in September 1940 and May 1941 as well as the blitz, with those awful bombings.

It was a different war where I was, watching the small fishing boats with no protection leave the quay. Women waved to the men leaving and I never gave it a thought that the sea was hazardous with mines, and who knows what might come out of the sea? I learnt after I left St. Ives that 1940-1941 was the worst year for fishermen, with the danger of their ships being hit by mines.

We learnt how to make fishing nets. One always hung on a door in the house for everyone to weave a line or two as they passed by. I did hear the news about the bombings in London and other places, but somehow buried it away in my mind, not being able to think of Mum and Dad being hurt away from me.

The beaches in St. Ives were very different from my local Southend-on-Sea seaside, or even Brighton where we used to go and visit Mum's sister, only an hour's run by train. Here in Cornwall, the streets were narrow, even the sounds were different, and I breathed salt air all the time.

I missed home, some days more than others, with a heart-wrenching thump, or a sickening feeling in the pit of my stomach. Home was a well known picture in my mind of old streets, some shabby areas but with front door steps scrubbed every day and the old brass letter boxes sparkling clean. I recalled the noise of that old school bell and the one the Muffin man rang on Saturday evenings.

I could hear in my mind, when I was feeling lonely, the shouts of the costermongers on Sunday mornings when they came down our streets pushing a wheelbarrow piled with cockles, winkles and mussels they brought from Leigh-on-Sea, and fish from other parts of the Essex coast. They had shrimps, too, on their barrows and I went with Mum out to the road to buy some for our Sunday tea. The costermonger women wore big flat hats or caps like their men. They stuck long steel hatpins in these so they were securely fastened. Their long skirts had a big, square apron tied on top and beneath this apron they had a canvas money bag where they stowed the money we gave them. (No one could steal it from them). Costermongers were usually known as selling fruit and veg. in the busy London markets. On Sundays they brought us these other tasty things to eat.

A picture of them and happy days was always with me. I never thought how changed things would be. I never realised how devastated our streets and docks were looking after nightly bombing raids. Home, I imagined, would always be the same, but it would be several years before I saw it again.

Suddenly it was Christmas. A big parcel arrived from London and I knew it was from Mum and Dad as they'd told me in a letter that it was in the post. I didn't open it until Christmas Day. We went to church with the Clares on Christmas morning and joined in singing the carols with gusto. Home to a meal then we opened the presents.

Doreen and I had saved our pocket money that we received regularly from home. We had bought small trinkets for Mr. and Mrs. Clare, little baubles in the market when we went there. I had made bookmarks for the two girls which I'd coloured. They bought us writing paper and envelopes. Doreen's parcel held books and a knitted hat. Mine contained a lovely knitted jumper in bright wool that my Mum had made, and some matching gloves for my birthday which was on the 29th. Dad's present to me for my birthday was a small leather bound English/French dictionary, signed in his beautiful copperplate handwriting. And for Christmas a picture he had drawn in charcoal of a blackbird. He had framed it in that tape they used then for framing photographs. I knew that he'd had trouble with his eyes and was pleased he could still use the talent he had, to draw such a beautiful picture. Their gifts seemed to bring them nearer to me. How I missed them. That dictionary, in which he'd put the date 1940, I used throughout my school life and I still have it near me.

We all sat round the fire and listened to the radio, then Rita tipped out a huge jigsaw puzzle that she had bought at the Wesleyan church Christmas fête and we all set to working on it, and Rita laughed and hoped there were no pieces missing. As I joined in the laughter I thought of my parents round the fire in our house in Plaistow and knew they would be thinking of me.

Chapter Two - Changes

Dedication

I dedicate the act of making bread
to the memory of my mother,
whose hands, too, turned flour over

while I, watching the easy movement
of her hands, noticed the small familiarity
of things, china jugs along the shelves
and tulips, like hanging lamps
bordering the window ledge.

Her hands, within the bowl's glazed depths,
became my daily pattern,
and now, turning flour to bread
I make a dedication.

Quite suddenly it all changed, or perhaps I grew up? This idyllic time in Cornwall came to an end. I mentioned that I had sat what was known as the scholarship exam. We took this when we were 11 and now the results had arrived and it seemed that most of us (my friends) were being split up. We were all going to different schools, some to the Grammar, myself to what was then called Central schools, the first of the technical colleges. Some went home, back to London too upset to stay away any longer. I had promised my parents to be brave and so I tried, hid the tears when I felt lonely, said my prayers and waited to be told when I would leave to go to the new school and I would be told then where this school was. I would be remaining in St. Ives for a little while, the headmistress told me.

Our school in St. Ives was a hall in the Wesleyan chapel where we went on Sundays with Mr. and Mrs. Clare. He had a very deep voice, and I loved to hear him singing the well known Wesley hymns. A respected local man, he owned a shop which sold tools and all things for do-it-yourself folk. He was known throughout the County, as not only did he give talks and workshops to the local St. John's Ambulance brigade but he had helped to rescue and resuscitate many from shipwrecks along that coast.

A wreck of one ship lay in the sea off our shore. This skeleton of a ship both fascinated and frightened me. With the other London children, I used to watch the sea break over it and imagine men struggling in the water. I was ignorant at that time of how, as the war continued, many more would lose their lives in the same way.

So now, having got to know this area a little and learning to love it, I had to leave. It wasn't only the place. I'd miss the people. I had come to know this new Aunt and Uncle and their family, a sort of second home for a while, where I felt not only cared for but loved. I wrote to my parents and I guess they were notified that I would be moving somewhere else. What it must have felt like for them I can't imagine. I felt numb. I knew it was something I had to do. I had grown a little older and my new school was somewhere far away. I was told what this could mean for my future, my education, my life!

What child of eleven or twelve considers that when she is to be uprooted yet again? My home in London seemed so far away. Mum and Dad were thankfully surviving, but suddenly the worries began. How long would they be safe? Where was my brother, out on those long convoys they'd told me about, was he safe? He'd been in a sea battle earlier in the war. He had been on board the H.M.S. Achilles that helped to fight a

German battleship, the Graf Spee, at the battle of the River Plate in December1939. Recently I'd heard on the news how bad the blitz had been in London and other places. I was thankful that my parents had survived, and was glad to hear that the bombings were now less frequent.

While we waited to learn about our moves to new schools and distant places, we played in the areas we'd come to know here in St. Ives. On fine days this was outside. Our outside was not the streets like at home in West Ham, but on a grassy area known as the island, or the beach. Just being there filled me with pleasure. The sun might not always shine, but the whole atmosphere of sand, sea, salt air, sounds of birds and smells of wild thyme and clover was for me a kind of heaven.

This didn't mean that I loved it more than my home town, but I knew St. Ives would be part of my mind and life forever. I didn't need a game to play or a ball to throw. Just to walk on the sand, or lie on it and absorb all around me with the sights and smells and sounds was simply incredible.

That August before we left St. Ives they held a fête. I'd been to church ones in London so I knew about them. I told Aunty Clare about them, how in the churches they had sales and bazaars, where there were tombolas and raffles with lots of prizes. She laughed at my excitement and said 'we have those here too.'

So I went on to tell her about the Sunday School outings, when we went to the countryside, Epping Forest, 'and we had donkey rides.' She laughed at my enthusiasm. So I continued telling her all I remembered about those trips. 'We were given sandwiches and lemonade, and Mum took me on a bus, a Greenline I think it was called, to Wanstead Flats to a big fair.' I stopped then in the middle of remembering and must have looked sad as I thought of Mum, because Aunty Clare gave me a big hug.

That expanse of green at Wanstead, with its lake where boys sailed their toy boats, had seemed a vast world to me then, but Cornwall, well St. Ives, had opened up a whole new universe to me.

In St. Ives the fête went on for a few days. Shop windows were decorated and coloured flags and bunting were tied across the narrow roads and all along the quayside and the sheds where we used to take our fishing nets for inspection after we'd finished them at home. I presumed they were for the men to take on their fishing trawlers when they pushed out to sea. I thought those fishermen were like heroes out of my story books, bronzed by the sea air and always giving us children a cheery smile.

I'd seen one of them save a young lad once down on the beach. The youngster had got into trouble in the sea. The alarm was raised, but the tide had dragged the lad far out. Several men went into the sea immediately, but one swam faster than them all. I saw the man reach the boy, turn him over and bring him back to the beach. Everyone rushed to the boy who was unconscious. Help was at hand with something resembling a see-saw that they manoeuvred the boy onto. I watched as they worked it just as you would a see-saw in a park. I saw him spew out a stream of greenish water. A great gasp went up from the watching crowd as they saw that the boy was alive.

I was turned away then by one of the adults. I noticed the rescuer was sitting nearby exhausted, panting, and with water still streaming from his body. Someone came to him with a blanket and a drink.

I felt pleased about that, for he had saved a life quickly and bravely. I knew that was a few moments in time that I would never forget. So much to remember from my days in St. Ives, and the summer fête was my final event there. It was fun, filled with swimming races for adults and children, raffles, and yes! a tombola like the ones I had seen at the church fêtes at home in London. In St. Ives fête we also had fishing for crabs, canoe rides and ice creams of all flavours.

Hot and cold pasties were always on hand. We'd

watched Aunty Clare making these when we'd first arrived. She'd put so much in them – diced veg and some onions for flavour, and beautiful pastry made the crust. She showed us how you turned it over and prinked the edge; lovely and tasty when made properly, and we ate them hot at home, or cold later on the beach. As I watched my new Aunty making the pastry I would recall my mother's hands handling flour in our big yellow china bowl as she made bread or cake. I longed for home then and the comfort of watching my mother doing this, but I never doubted that I would go home and see her and Dad again.

Perhaps because it was a beautiful summer that year, I was always as full of joy as I could be. Oh! I missed Mum and Dad and home and the familiar ways like the big, bustling weekend markets. Mum and I used to go to the local one in Queen's Road, Upton Park, on a Saturday afternoon. We could buy groceries at our corner shop, but it was in the market that we bought cheap dresses (for me), and bags and other things, like hairbrushes and bits of jewellery that glittered brightly under those hanging lamps that were lit when the market stayed open late, and the jellied eel shops in competition with each other. Some Sundays Dad took me to Petticoat Lane and Club Row, farther along in the east end, nearer Whitechapel and Mile End.

Dad loved his London, born and bred in Plaistow, West Ham, where we now lived. He told me tales of how he remembered it as being countryside with some open cattle markets. He had been orphaned aged eleven and went to work then in another market. I remember him telling me this as he sat in his oak chair by the fire and I curled up on the fender seat by his side. 'The law had just been changed by Parliament,' he said, 'and boys of my age could no longer be sent to work up chimneys as chimney sweep boys.' I shuddered at the thought of small boys being pushed inside those soot filled places where they found it hard to breathe.

Dad's married sister brought him up. He was pleased she did as otherwise he would have had to go to what they called 'The Ragged School'. It was nearby where we lived, although no longer a school for orphan boys. Yes, I missed being at home and listening to my Mum and Dad and their tales of the past. In Cornwall, however, I had found a second home and people who cared for me. My mind was awash with joy that day of the fête in St. Ives, and lingering on happy memories of me and Mum in London markets, and Dad with his pride of Plaistow.

The fête in St. Ives was my farewell to Cornwall. Doreen was excited about going to her new school, but more excited about going home first, back to West Ham for a few weeks before travelling to her secondary school. The school which I would have to go to was quite a long way away, and it was thought best that I went straight there by train. I was to learn afterwards that my Dad, whose eyes had been injured in an accident at work before I was born, had been receiving treatment and now had to have an operation in London Eye Hospital, and what with the anxiety of that and the sudden bombing raids it was a worrying time for my parents.

When I think back, I realise the anguish they must have felt, desperate to see me and yet having to cope with my father's operation plus the concern about bombing raids, however less frequent. I can imagine them, talking long into the nights about whether to have me home. They were being brave and I had promised them that I would be brave too. So when I was eventually told by my headmistress that I was going to my new school shortly and that it was in the County of Wiltshire, I felt quite resigned. I would never forget St. Ives and all the lovely people I had met there, but because of this war I had to travel far away to my new school.

Chapter Three - Lost

Waiting to be Met
(An evacuee - 1940)

A child, too big to cry
I'd grown up in that year of war,
'was old enough' they said
to travel far, loneliness, a familiar friend,
came with me. The guard had helped me
to descend, unloading bag and me, clutching
my gas-mask in its cardboard box, the pocket game.
He'd asked, in his country drawl,
'You know her name?'
He meant the woman coming to collect me.
No-one came.

The silence was immense
after the train had gone;
late sunlight daubed the wooden seat,
the picket fence, against which I leant
too big to cry, and waited.
No-one came.

I thought I heard a clock chime five
tolling into emptiness and fear;
then footsteps hurrying near, and through the gate
the woman came, unsmiling,
to take me to her home.
I stayed two years, but even now,
it seems upon reflection, that
no-one ever came at Trowbridge Station.

The sun was still shining and the seagulls still making a noise on rooftops the day I left St. Ives to go to my new home and new school. My favourite teacher was coming to the station with me, so all the Clares, except their son still away in the R.A.F., lined up by the front door to say goodbye. Mrs. Clare, whom I had come to love, gave me a big hug. Rita, their eldest daughter, gave me her book *The Golden Treasury of Verse*. She signed it 'with love from Rita'. Taking it, near to tears, I told her 'I will keep it always,' and it is still with me.

I didn't understand any of it, in fact I felt a bit muddled about things. I had lived in West Ham, East London, where home and everything was familiar. I knew all the streets so well. I knew the little shops and the markets and my school and friends. It had been very strange being an evacuee but I had become used to the little winding streets in St. Ives, the small shops, most of all, the home with Mr. and Mrs. Clare.

School was a different building but my teachers were the ones who had travelled from London with me. Quite soon, the wonderful beaches, the sea and new friends became familiar. And then there were the home made pasties and the glorious thick Cornish ice cream which you bought at the local shop, and chose thin or thick layers to put in the bowl you took. All things so different from my home life, but all of which, during my time in this lovely place, I had come to not only accept, but to enjoy.

I knew the move was because I had passed the scholarship and that meant going to a new school which was in another part of England, in another county called Wiltshire. I felt gripped by some imaginable fear. I didn't know what I had to be afraid of, but that fear was there. Perhaps it was because, yet again, I was facing the unknown.

My lovely teacher and a railway guard saw me onto the train. The carriage was full, but a place had been reserved for me. No other children came with me, just grown ups in the seats and all strangers. As the train pulled away I glanced back through the window and I was convinced that I saw Mrs. Clare watching from behind an iron barrier. It was the last time I was to see her.

I had been told the name of my new school. It was Russell Central School, and I would have a new uniform, but it hadn't arrived before I left St. Ives, so it should be going to my new billet, wherever that would be.

I had my case and a bag of refreshments that Mrs. Clare had carefully packed for me. I had another small bag which held some drawing books and coloured pencils. I remember feeling stiff with nervous tension and couldn't at first concentrate to do any drawing or colouring. I had a book and some comics, but I just sat and stared in front of me as the train gathered speed. The people in the carriage were friendly and tried to chat with me, but I was, and I don't know why, strangely hostile and openly rude to them.

Remembering it all now, I believe I was upset by leaving those I loved for the second time, and angry towards those people in the train with me because they spoke about going to their homes. I didn't know where home was, I felt quite lost.

It was a long journey. Nowadays a train from St. Ives to Trowbridge takes five and a half hours. I guess it took much longer in 1940. I didn't feel tired, and in the end I did talk a little to the others in the carriage. 'I'm going to a new school,' I told them, and they praised me when I said I had passed the scholarship. 'I haven't got my new uniform yet,' I mentioned. Obviously I was concerned about this. They tried to reassure me, but nothing would ease this fear I had, although I felt proud to be able to tell them that I knew the name of the County I was going to and the place which was Trowbridge. 'No,' I said, 'I don't know where it is on a map.' Once or twice the guard on the train came to make sure that I was all right.

When I heard the name 'Trowbridge, Trowbridge station' being called out I gathered up my coat, case and bags.

A guard opened the carriage door for me, and helped me down onto the platform. Then I stood alone and watched the train steam away from me. The sun beat down on me as I stood and waited. It was hot but I felt numb, frozen with that awful fear. It was very quiet. A pigeon fluttered along nearby and that was the only sound I heard until in the distance a clock chimed five. I imagined it was coming from some church tower.

I put my case down and my bags and leant against the little wooden fence that led to a road outside the station. I don't know how long I stood there. I didn't know what to do, so I went back onto the small platform. Suddenly I heard footsteps coming the other way and a woman came hurrying towards me. 'I'm late,' she said, unsmiling.

My fear still clutched me but I managed a small 'Hallo.'

She picked up my case and began walking. 'Hurry,' she said sharply, glancing back at me over her shoulder. I gathered up my small bags and joined her. She told me her name, Mrs. Price, and the road where she lived, 'Which isn't far,' she said, 'but I have to be home to get Celia and Jane's tea. They're my daughters,' she explained. 'Celia's older than you and Jane is nearly eight.' I didn't really take it in, I was confused and very tired by now. I paused to take a drink from the bottle of water in my bag. She seemed to get more sympathetic when she saw me doing this. 'You'll have tea with the girls when we get home,' she assured me.

The walk to her house seemed a long way. On one side of the road we turned into there were a few terraced houses. I was to learn that they were farm labourers homes. I was in the country now and not by the sea. The fields on the other side of the road seemed to stretch into the skyline. I was walking more slowly when she got a little more chatty. 'You from London?' she asked suddenly. I nodded then she went on, 'I've not had an evacuee before. Others here have, all from London, but they didn't want any more dirty Londoners.' I took a deep breath but didn't know how to reply. Then she said the words that truly made me feel unwanted. 'They've paid me extra, they couldn't find another billet.' Looking back now I think it may have been some sort of compliment that she would actually take me in, even if I was a dirty Londoner.

I was still silent when we arrived at her house. It had a long front garden path to the front door, and the few houses either side were all the same. An older girl opened the door for us. 'I'm Celia,' she said brusquely. I learnt later that she was in her last year at secondary school, so a few years older than me. A big girl, she seemed to tower over me. The younger one, her sister, kept behind her watching this strange new arrival, their evacuee.

Mrs. Price took me to a small room up the little stairs that opened out, it seemed, from what I had thought was a cupboard door. Once at the top of them I saw there was a window on the landing and two or three other bedrooms. After a wash downstairs in what was the scullery I sat down at a big wooden table in what they used as their main room. I had ham and egg with them, and Mr. Price came in later from work. He seemed as gruff as Mrs. Price, but spoke kindly when I said goodnight and went to unpack. I went to bed early, thankful that I had arrived safely in Trowbridge. I said my prayers as I always did and fell into a deep sleep.

I know Mum and Dad were notified quickly that I had arrived. Maybe a telegram was sent, but I was told that they knew. I don't think anyone notified Mr. and Mrs. Clare in St. Ives, and I felt strangely numb about it all and just got on with what had to come next, like getting to know the place where I lived, and where did I go to school and how did I get there?

Another worry was that my new school uniform still hadn't arrived. Of course post was very much delayed in those war years, priority given to more serious matters than delivery of my school uniform. I woke early and jumped out of bed to pull the curtains back and look out onto what was obviously the back garden of this house. A long path, between rows of what I presumed were vegetables, led to railings which separated the garden from the field at the end.

The room I had been given was comfortable with somewhere to hang my clothes and a small chest of drawers for other things, a chair, no bookshelf, but I put the few books I had on top of the chest of drawers. There was also a wooden bedside table with a little oil light. I washed in the scullery and cleaned my teeth. Mrs. Price was brewing tea and spoke quite kindly to me. 'Jane's out with her Dad,' she told me. 'She often goes with him on Saturdays, Celia will take you into town later, and tomorrow,' she went on, 'she'll show you where your school is.' Celia was sitting at the big dining table eating toast, and didn't look too happy at the prospect of taking me around, but I would be glad to know how to get to my new school. I did manage to eat some toast and honey while Celia poured the tea.

I was told by Mrs. Price to help Celia clear the dishes and wash up with her. My coat had been hung on some hooks in the passage that led to the front door, and Celia now told me to put it on and we'd go for a walk to town. I did as I was told, eager to see what Trowbridge was like. Outside the air was fresh and on the opposite side of the road was a field with what looked like cabbages growing. I guessed they were, as everyone had been encouraged to grow what they could because food would be in short supply.

The air did not have the salty freshness of Cornwall, and although Celia wasn't very chatty I told her a little of what St. Ives had been like. 'It'll be different for you here then,' was her comment. I asked if they'd had other children staying with them, but she sniffed and repeated what her mother had said, 'We didn't want them.' This time she did not mention about 'dirty Londoners' and I was relieved, already making up my mind that I would prove to them that I was not dirty.

There were various shops in the small town she led me into. All the usual ones; a baker's where people were queuing outside. 'They're waiting for lardy cake,' Celia told me.

Curious, I asked 'What's that?'

'Don't you know?' she scoffed, something that she was to do a lot, I was to discover. I learnt about lardy cake as time went on, and it was delicious, I found, but in short supply now. There was a Woolworths; I remember writing to Mum and Dad and telling them how small it was. There was a small green area the other side of the shops and in the distance was a large building. 'That's the Town Hall,' Celia told me when I asked. That place was to play an important part in my life during my stay in Trowbridge. I was already missing the quaint cobbled streets of St. Ives, and the sea air and the noisy seagulls.

Back at the house Jane and her father had returned. 'Been ferreting,' he told me. I had no idea what he meant, but didn't like to ask. I wandered out with Jane into the garden. There was nowhere to play as it was all turned over to vegetables, as were all the other gardens on either side. I peered through the railings at the end of the path. The field had nothing planted in it. When I asked Jane who it belonged to, she told me it was owned by a farmer. As the months passed I heard the expression 'lying fallow' when people spoke about fields that were not cultivated.

Sunday, the Prices didn't go to any church. I went out with both girls. Jane was still only at early school and there was a big age gap between her and her sister, but they seemed to get on well. Celia felt her importance when she took me to where my school was. It was a hall of some sort, locked, of course, as it was Sunday. By stretching up on my toes I could just see inside through one of the windows. It looked a vast space with trestle tables along the width of it. Celia told me with triumph in her voice, as she was a bit of a bully, 'You'll be the new girl in first year and you won't know anyone!' I tried not to show that she upset me.

Once home I wrote a long letter to Mum and Dad.

Missing them was almost a physical pain, and writing to them was the best I could do to ease the pain. That night in my bedroom I prayed that the war would soon end so that I could return to my real home in London.

The postman didn't bring my school uniform in time for me to wear it to my new school. Prior to starting there one of the teachers, a Miss Smithson, called at my billet one Sunday afternoon. She asked Mrs. Price and me if all was well, and was I settled in? What could I reply other than 'Yes, thank you'? She had a kind face and told me that I would feel a little strange at first because the others were older than me and had moved with the Central School in the first evacuation, like herself, so they were quite established there. She smiled as she said all this. She was a sort of self appointed housemistress, and I would be in her class for English and French and some other things. My mind couldn't take it all in. She told me not to worry about my school uniform not arriving. I was touched by her thoughtfulness to come and make sure that all was well with me. Because of her visit I resolved to work hard at school.

Chapter Four - Recognition

Embarkation

It was the country 'safe' they'd said from bombs.
I woke at the time of frosted light -
saw rows of armoured vehicles in the field beyond.

Neat stooks of rifles, tents, and men who moved
like shadows, passing beneath the window
of my room, carrying accoutrements of war
while I, unobserved, watched the steady to and fro
until a whistle shrilled, and they ran
doubled up in rows.

An evacuee, instructed not to talk,
I passed them on my way to school. One called,
his accent was my own. I waited,
feeling the ache in me begin,
the too familiar sense of longing; he plodded
through furrows frosted deep, and hard
as the iron railings round the field.
He spoke of home, showed me photographs
of wife and son, his breath made small clouds
between us. From the house they shouted,
called me in, wordlessly I thrust the pictures back.

His homesickness was my own.
The field looked desolate when they had gone.

I was right, starting my new school without the required uniform was awful. When it still hadn't arrived in time for me to start the term I had no one to tell me what I should wear instead. So I wore my dark plaid skirt, a white blouse and navy blue cardigan. So, not the usual gymslip or the clip-on bow tie, and not the hat with the Russell school badge on the front.

All eyes were turned in my direction when, at the morning assembly, I was introduced to the school by the headmaster. I felt certain that everyone was laughing at me, and to make matters worse I was the only first former to have arrived.

Another thing that didn't make for a happy start for me was the fact that there was a war going on between two of the upper form girls, both of whom thought they should be head girl. Whenever there was a suitable opportunity, girls would gather in small groups and discuss who they should vote for. I was dragged into making a choice although I didn't know either of the girls concerned. The choice I made didn't please the other tribe, as I thought of them, and some stopped speaking to me, while books got knocked off my part of the trestle table. At playtimes and lunch break I got knocked roughly aside. Whoever said that 'school days are your best' lied!

At home I tried to tell Celia about it, but she was at a local school with its own complicated politics and barely listened. Little Jane was too young to understand, but she did play games with me and did jigsaw puzzles we set up on a table that Mrs. Price said we could use.

Things gradually settled at school, and other first years arrived, which was more company for me. Two first formers were boys who were in the Grove Central school. This school had merged with mine, the Russell, as we were a little depleted in numbers. Russell colours were blue, the Grove was red. These two boys had red caps which I admired.

My uniform had finally arrived but I was disappointed.

The gymslip was too long and so were the sleeves of my new shirts. The hat, a sort of soft pillbox, I wore pulled down low on my brow and got laughed at by the other girls. They did show me, however, the way to put a tuck in the back of it so that it sat back on my head more.

Gradually I began to get accepted, but still felt lonely. Always a bookish child, I turned more and more to reading for comfort. The two Grove school boys were friends who were billeted together in a house a long way down Bradford Road. This was the main road to Bradford-on-Avon. It was also the road where I lived, so we walked home together after school.

The boys pulled off their caps on the way home and tossed them about, kicking them along the road and laughing. I envied them being able to live together as I missed Doreen's company. My new friends told me that they'd been teased by the local lads because they didn't know anything about country ways. However, they'd been able to show off because they had come straight from London and had been in the blitz. They could boast about this to the country boys and tell them about the bombs they'd seen, and show the shrapnel they had collected on the bomb sites. Their houses had only been damaged, they told me, and I reminded myself how lucky I had been to avoid all that.

I became happier at school. Other first years arrived and I made friends. We shared laughter in unexpected ways, like the times when under Miss Smithson's eyes we did needlework, mainly darning the thick lisle stockings we wore and which were difficult to replace. There was a time when she decided we should, for a short while, do this while wearing our gasmasks. It's hard to breathe when those rubber masks are put on, so we took it in turns to slip under the trestle table where we worked and slip the mask off. I guess Miss Smithson could hear us giggling as we did so, but she let it pass. Ethel, my classmate, wore glasses, and when it was her turn to slip under the table we giggled again as her glasses misted inside the eye piece of the gasmask. It's just as well we didn't really need to use those masks.

We had packed lunches, and it was at these times that we all told each other where we'd been, some from other counties, some from London. I longed to talk about London and home. I heard regularly from Mum and Dad and they seemed to be coping; at least they always said they were all right. My longing for them didn't go away, however much laughter I might have had at school.

Home life was bearable, I had good food, kept clean, but something was missing. I guess it was the family love I'd had. Celia bullied me verbally, she belittled my accent, and once or twice when her parents were out she gave me a slight blow or knock if I answered her back. It never occurred to me that she might be jealous, not for anything I could do better than her, but because I was an intruder in her close knit family. Jane, her sister, was father's pet. She'd explained about the ferreting to me, and how they put one of these creatures into a rabbit hole and the poor frightened rabbit shot out into a snare, a sort of wire hoop, she told me. 'Did it kill the rabbit?' I wanted to know.

As a girl brought up in the country and knowing about these things, she laughed at me. 'Yes!' she exclaimed, 'Dad always gets one at least.' He was to show us his 'kill' one Sunday morning. He made us all go into the scullery near the big stone sink. The dead rabbit he laid on the draining board was going to be skinned. The little thing's neck was broken from the snare, and it flopped as he laid it down.

If he hoped to shock this city girl he was wrong. I stood strangely fascinated as he told us how 'you pull the skin up to the head, then over the top, over the head and tug hard and the head snaps off.' I didn't tell him that my mother was originally a country woman and knew how to skin a rabbit. She would buy an unskinned rabbit cheaper from a butcher, bring it home and skin it neatly herself. I'd watched her do this, but let him think he was showing off to this evacuee from London town. The culture here in Trowbridge was different from the one I'd known at St. Ives, and both of them varied from the London life I'd known before becoming an evacuee.

Because we were living in the country we were taken on nature walks. They were very good actually. Mr. Ames, our art teacher and the boys' maths teacher, took us on some of these. He told us about the beechnuts that fell, and once we saw the skin that a snake had shed. We picked various leaves and took them back to draw and paint pictures of.

One time he took us to see the White Horse that is carved in the chalk of Westbury Hill. I think we had use of transport to take us all there. It was a bright day; the country views were clear. For the first time I appreciated being there, and we were allowed to walk round the horse, now camouflaged by nets daubed in the surrounding colours, so that any enemy aircraft couldn't spot it as a landmark. I was proud to walk round it and Mr. Ames told us it was threequarters of a mile altogether, that walk. Again, when I look back I realise how good the teachers were at finding things for our education and entertainment.

Mr. Price knew where to look for things in the countryside too, and when we went with him he showed us different mushrooms and fungi. One day he spotted a tiny wild flower known as a bee orchid, because it is a miniature orchid and resembles a bee. He let me pick one which I took into school and got commended for finding it, but it was really Mr. Price who had known where to look for it. He worked in a factory where they did something with wool. The wool was necessary for making uniforms, and I guess other clothes including my gymslip.

One day when he came in from work he told us that people were being asked to pick teasels. These could be seen growing in damp areas beside ponds and lakes. A machine had broken down in his factory. It was German so no parts could be obtained. Without this machine they could not card or comb the raw wool supplied to them. In medieval times, the teasels were used by hand to comb the raw wool. 'We'll do this at work now for a particular part of the process of combing the wool,' Mr. Price proudly explained. Once again, I had learnt about a different culture because I was in a different part of the country. It seemed far removed from my old London life.

I heard from the news that the country was in a difficult position as regards to food and other things. Many things were on ration and we had special ration cards for foodstuffs, which had to be shown in the shops. I don't remember being hungry as we seemed to have just enough to keep us sustained. Petrol had been rationed early in the war. In 1940 bacon, butter and sugar were also put on rations, closely followed by other things like meat, tea, jam, biscuits, cheese, eggs, lard and milk. More would follow. I understood now why everyone had been asked to grow vegetables, and parks were being dug up to allow for this. The contributions Mr. Price occasionally made by his ferreting helped with our meat supply in Bradford Road, Trowbridge.

Conscription had reduced the number of school teachers we had. Mr. Ames was, I guessed, above the age for call up, and so was Miss Smithson. Miss Johnson was younger. She was our French teacher who also sometimes took my class for geography. She also took physical education and games, and arranged for us to have some tennis lessons in a local court. I really enjoyed these as the rough and tumble of netball was not to my liking. Once a young man in army uniform came to visit her. We saw her walking with him sometimes after school in the nearby countryside. How foolish we young teenagers were. We giggled when we saw them. Who knows? He may have been on embarkation leave. Shortly after Miss Johnson left us. I think she had been conscripted too.

We were getting through the autumn now, and those beechnuts and leaves Mr Ames had shown us how to collect were being made into brooches and pins for Christmas presents. Under his guidance we varnished the beechnuts so that they glowed, painted some other things he'd found for us, other sorts of nuts. These he showed us how to paint in various colours that didn't rub off. He helped us bind them in tiny bunches to make a brooch, and had special clips to stick on the back of each brooch as fasteners. Whether he brought a supply with him, or if he was able to obtain these things I don't know, but we all had fun making them. We also painted special paper which he called parchment, first cutting it into carefully measured strips to make bookmarks. The harder we worked in his art classes the more presents we made.

It was a splendid autumn, perhaps because I was noticing the change of colour in my surroundings, as leaves turned yellows and gold. Sometimes there was a mist in the mornings. One morning before school, as Mrs. Price got our breakfast and packed lunches ready, she asked 'Did anyone hear the noise last night?' We shook our heads. 'Wondered if you did as you sleep in the back.' Her enquiry was to me. I shook my head. 'Go and look then.' She shooed us out of the back door.

Celia was first at the railings at the end of the garden. 'Soldiers,' she called out before hurrying back indoors. I stood with Jane looking through the railings that had early morning frost dripping from them.

After Jane left I stood a while longer taking in the scene of the ploughed up field, ploughed up by the army vehicles that had come in overnight. Everywhere there were stocks of rifles with tents and soldiers hurrying about. The hum of their voices drifted across, and one of them wandered up to me. 'Is that where you live?' He nodded towards the house behind me.

I knew his accent was the same as mine, so I told him, 'No, I'm an evacuee from London.'

He smiled from ear to ear. 'Me too.'

He started to tell me where he was from when Mrs. Price called out 'Doris, come in now. Time for school.' I left him, happy to have met up with someone from my part of the world.

I hurried home that afternoon after school, hoping to talk with that soldier once more. To my amazement the field was empty, just the rutted soil where the vehicles had torn at it savagely. Everything was gone, tents had disappeared and those rifles. It was raining a little, an autumn evening was coming in, the field look desolate, and suddenly I realised that the soldier I had spoken to that morning felt as lonely as I did. He, too, had to leave his home in London. As I walked slowly back up the garden path and went in for my tea, I wondered where he and all the other soldiers had gone.

Chapter Five - Growing Up

Three haiku

Here inside my head
a world all my own, not yours,
but I am lonely.

What are all the words?
Drops of crystal purity
and recollections.

School days and memories
are entangled in my thoughts
term times, home time, love.

The Autumn in Trowbridge seemed to be moving along quickly. I guess it was because I had made more friends and knew my way around better.

That autumn there were two things that I especially enjoyed. One was the communal gathering of lots of local folk to pick hips from the hedgerows, or from those locally grown. We had been asked to do this by the government because fresh fruits, particularly oranges, were not now being imported from other countries. Our convoys at sea were being torpedoed or hit by mines laid by the enemy. Essential food was rationed, but it was to be a long while before we saw oranges and bananas and other fruits on sale again. Without fruit we were lacking the essential vitamin C, and rose hips contained a valuable source of this. With many of my friends we searched nearby hedgerows for the ripest rose hips. There was a main central point where we could leave our collected berries. This was the local W.I. hall where the tables on collection day were full of jars of these red rose hips.

Another enjoyment for me was that I had heard, through girls at school, that a local Guide Troop was held each week in Trowbridge Town Hall. I wrote to Mum and asked if she could send my guide uniform, just the tunic, leather belt and tie; no need to send the hat, I'd told her, knowing with its big brim and crown it would be difficult to fit into a parcel. It took a little while for this to arrive as posts were a bit delayed, but since women were now being used to replace the postmen who had been conscripted, things had improved.

I was excited when I arrived home from school one day to find the parcel from London had been delivered. Inside was a loving letter from Mum and Dad, with, of course, my Guide tunic, which I would wear with my navy skirt, and the belt plus the tie, a triangular piece of material which could double up as a bandage if required. This had to be folded correctly and tied at the back of the neck with a reef knot (still remember the sort of mantra I went round saying to learn how to do it – 'Right over left, left over right and under'.)

This and the other knots I'd learnt enabled me to win my first badge which, with Mum's help, I had managed to stitch onto my sleeve and wear with pride. One night, late autumn, I joined the Trowbridge Girl Guides where I was made very welcome by the Captain and Lieutenant, and of course some of my school friends were there.

Trowbridge, the house where I was billeted and a new school all seemed very strange at first, but those Guide nights were something familiar. They followed the usual pattern of patrol games and singsongs. I worked hard for new badges and achieved those of Bird Lover, Musician, Athlete and Book Lover. This, together with school life, kept me reasonably happy.

There was no camping during this time, but we were quite often taken out on day treks by our Guiders. One was waiting to be called up, and one was working in a factory in a reserved occupation, so she would not be conscripted. Saturday was the day we went on these trips, this because of school and the employment days of our two Guiders. We carried food and plimsolls, (what we now call trainers), in our rucksacks.

Our compass reading was put to good use on these trips. We townies learnt a lot about wild flowers, insects and birds. The Captain and colleague and other volunteer helpers brought Billy cans, and water was usually made available at a farm where the guiders had made arrangements to call and settle in one of their fields.

We were taught how to light a camp fire and the water was boiled in cans, supplied by a couple of senior scouts, to make cups of tea. Frying pans were mysteriously produced and sausages spluttered and sizzled as we cooked them on the open fire. We had to clean up afterwards, including the fire, and leave no trace of our having been there. We had great fun on these occasions and returned home dirty and tired, but a sense of happiness about all of that stayed with me.

In their letter Mum and Dad said they would love to send me some sweets, but there were none available of course. The war was taking its toll; so many houses had been damaged. Their house had survived, but some nearby had been blasted and patched up in a temporary way with tarpaulin over walls and roofs, and cardboard placed at windows where glass had been blown out. And they were sorry to say that some of the houses while in this condition had been burgled. I couldn't imagine what the streets must look like now, especially as they told me that some of the bombsites had been dug over and vegetables were now grown there.

As well as our berry gathering, lots of things were being done to help the war effort. Wherever possible people were growing what food they could. There were long queues outside shops whenever it got known that something was available, like certain meats and greengrocery. Rationing meant each person had so many points to use on certain items. It had been worked out carefully, and statistics showed that the points system was sufficient for each individual. Bread remained unrationed throughout the war, as did fish and chips.

At Guides we were encouraged to knit. We made scarves, gloves and socks for the armed forces. We collected old newspapers and, when we found it, silver foil, all taken to a central point and put to special use.

One Guide night, to our surprise, a fishing net was draped over the floor in the room where we met. This, the Captain told us, was a template, 'And on it,' she pointed out, 'there are areas marked in different colours.' Dark and light green, black and shades of brown were predominant. We collected from a table strips of material called hessian, each piece approximately two feet long and two inches wide. These were dyed in the same colours as marked on the fishing net. It was our job, Captain explained, to 'Crawl on the floor and tie these pieces to the corresponding colours on the net.' Each strip had to be tied and knotted tightly.

We did this with enthusiasm, not just for the fun of it, but because Captain told us we were making camouflage nets which would help to disguise guns, tents, tanks, and all manner of things. I was proud to tell Captain and the group that I had helped to make the actual nets whilst an evacuee in Cornwall.

The hessian, made from jute, was oily and smeared our hands and uniforms. The dye from the different colours rubbed off and tainted our fingers. It didn't matter, we were helping the war effort. The oily, dusty smells mingled with the fish and chip supper the Captain always brought on these occasions.

We did this once a month for some time, and oh! how I enjoyed those evenings. I wiped my oily and greasy hands on my handkerchief and sometimes, I must confess, down my

Guide tunic. I never gave a thought to the washing I was taking back for Mrs. Price, and although I never felt that her house in Trowbridge was my real home, she never complained about the washing she did for me, or the food she cooked and gave me.

The months went by. I didn't dislike school; it was a place where the others there had the same accent as me, like that soldier in the field at the bottom of the garden where I lived. So at school it was a bit of 'home'. I don't think I really worked at the lessons as much as I should, or could. I tackled what I was told to do. We didn't have much homework. What little we were given I usually managed to return. My marks were not in the highest grades, but I coped and mainly enjoyed each day there.

We were mixed classes, and boys were in an area in that big room, the hall, away from the girls. The teachers kept tight control over us, no mixing even at break times. Sometimes we had music lessons together, and with Christmas ahead a choir was formed. Jokes and laughter were shared on this occasion, and even the teachers joined in. It was mainly carols being rehearsed, but there were some good voices among us, both boys and girls, and a few of these were rehearsing solos to perform at a small concert when we broke up for Christmas.

It was at these times that my mind drifted back to London. We'd have had a concert at school and parents would come, I thought. It was no good, you had to shrug that thought away and get on with the time in hand. I remember telling Mum and Dad that I would be brave, and so I was. Any crying when I was sad, I did at night in my bed in Bradford Road, Trowbridge.

The nights were drawing in but I still got to Guides evenings. We were still making the camouflage nets. One night when a few of us were kneeling on the floor tying on the strips of dyed hessian there was a heavy bump, and the Town Hall seemed to judder a bit. 'What was that?' we wanted to know, but even when Captain went out for the fish and chips, she said no one knew what it had been.

The next day we found out. That heavy bump had been a bomb dropping on a village just outside Trowbridge. It seemed that bombers returning from raids had dropped their bombs, and some houses and a factory had been damaged. I was not told if anyone had been injured or killed, and I never heard, but Celia and Jane and myself would eventually be taken to see the large crater that the bomb had made. It measured 25ft across and was 12ft deep. The Kennet & Avon Canal ran along certain areas nearby and it had been made a fortified line of defence with pill boxes, etc., in case of invasion. Perhaps this was why the bomb had been dropped at that point. Whatever the reason, we had certainly heard it that evening in the Town Hall. How ironic, that I had been sent from London to avoid the bombing, and one had landed near where I now lived as an evacuee!

We had our concert at school the afternoon we broke up. Anyone could come and listen to us sing. The Prices didn't come, Mrs. Price was too busy and Mr. Price was at work, Jane and Celia had things to do at their own schools. I enjoyed the afternoon and the carols and hurried home.

There was great excitement for me as a parcel had arrived from London, which I opened to find presents wrapped up and not to be opened until Christmas Day! These gifts were wrapped in newspaper, as brown paper and tissue were difficult to obtain. By hoarding our food ration coupons, Mrs. Price had managed to get a very small joint of meat for the Christmas meal, and that together with a chicken from a neighbour who kept them in her garden meant we would have a good supply of meat over the holiday. The veg, of course, was freshly sourced from our own garden; brussels and carrots with the potatoes, and we would eat well. I hoped Mum and Dad were able to do the same.

Their gifts to me had been knitted items, a cardigan and two scarves, one for school in plain navy and the other in bright colours. I think a lot of women now were unpicking other woollen items and making up new things from the wool that they rewound and sometimes washed. They'd included a comic, and I'd said in my letters that I was writing poetry so some pencils and pens came in a little wooden box and some paper, and my Dad had written in his beautiful copperplate handwriting, 'for the poems'. It's true I was thinking up poems. I went round saying the lines I'd thought of, and was teased a lot for it by Celia.

The week prior to Christmas Mrs.Price polished and buffed everything. She was a houseproud woman. One morning each week she had us put the dining chairs on top of the table, and we had to polish their legs as well as the seats. Then all the ornaments had to be thoroughly dusted, all this while she beat and brushed carpets and mats.

There were few Christmas decorations. I think a line or two of home made coloured ones were put in the dining room. A small tree of some sort was brought in by Mr. Price, not a real Christmas tree, but a bit of tinsel twinkled on it when they lit a fire in the hearth on Christmas day. We did have a lovely dinner, but what's the word I can use to describe that Christmas? Drab. That's the way I thought of it, and possibly it wasn't, but it was very different from what I had known in London, and in St. Ives. As I have said, I was well fed, and my clothes always washed and ironed. I guess I missed the love of the home I'd been in until the wretched war!

Anyway Christmas dinner arrived and I had a piece of meat with a large amount of fat, which I quickly tried to remove, but Mr. Price would have none of it. 'Eat every bit, Doris,' he chided me, 'there's a war on you know!' As if I didn't know! That's why I was living with him in his house, because of a war. I didn't answer him, but struggled through the piece of fat. It's small things like that as much as the big things that bring the pain of homesickness. Mum knew how I hated the taste of fat, and she would have let me leave it.

Something similar happened later that Christmas day. We were round the fire and Mr. Price produced a small pottery jar, or it may have been a coloured tin, of ginger. He told us all to take a piece. 'A real treat,' he said proudly. I had never tasted ginger, so eager to try it I put a lump in my mouth and immediately knew that I hated it. I knew we were lucky to have it, things like this were so difficult to get and he must have gone to a lot of trouble to find it. I had learnt by then that it was sometimes necessary to be cunning. I went into the pantry on the pretence of getting something for the table and slipped the offending piece of this horrid stuff into my handkerchief then popped it into the pocket on my cardigan. A memorable Christmas!

Chapter Six - A Happiness

My Father

He watched the curves and straights
of all my writing,
hoping one day for magnificence,
like seeing water changed into wine.

His angularity in the small room
was strangely comforting.
He left me space to search through silences
allowing words to come uncrowded on the page,
and time was an unhurried walk into a garden.

Then later, he jogged my memory
with song, lines from poems and the psalms,
he waited, accepting the stridence of my adolescence.

Little by little, applying my pen,
I scrabbled through syllables, rhythms and words,
never quite managing a miracle.

Even without his presence in my room,
I have the (secret) sense that writing symbols,
plucking at lines and phrases, turning them around,
might somehow achieve something remarkable.

I felt I slid into the new year, not literally, but a slow
progression during the school holidays. Bad weather meant

days indoors in the warm, reading and writing letters home, I don't remember writing to my friend Doreen who had decided to stay in London and not return anywhere as an evacuee.

So days went slowly by. They were dull, cold days. Mind you, whenever I think back now to my evacuee days, memories of Cornwall bring thoughts of sunshine and clear skies, while Wiltshire conjures up for me images of grey skies and cold weather. This may be entirely in my mind, but that's how I remember that time in my life.

Everywhere then it seemed there was a sense of apprehension, or so I thought. We were in a worrying time of the war. I had heard all the news in June, about Dunkirk and how the country had managed to turn a defeat into that victory of bringing our armed forces back home. Again, I knew how in July through to September 1940 we had been defended by our brave airmen in the Battle of Britain.

Mum mentioned that one of my cousins, Johny, now in the infantry, had been wounded. I guessed it was at Dunkirk. I thought back to the times I had played after school round at Johny's house, as he had a sister and a brother nearer my age and they didn't live far from me in Plaistow. There were two others also, another girl and a boy who was just a baby. None of them had been evacuated, I think for fear of being separated and sent to different homes.

After the Christmas holidays it was back to school, where time passed more quickly. I didn't dislike school, only the maths lessons. I came into my own when we had English and literature. When called upon to write essays I excelled – about the only lesson in which I did! And if called upon to recite poetry, mine was the first hand that shot up to volunteer.

One murky Saturday afternoon Mr and Mrs Price said that a neighbour, who had a lorry, was taking us all to see that bomb crater, 'The one that dropped that night you were at Guides,' Mrs. Price told me.

So off we went. It was quite a trip for us. There were

not many folk with cars of any sort then, and if they had cars, petrol had been rationed since the beginning of the war. Once out from the lorry Celia and Jane ran, me with them, over the field to where we were told we would see the crater. 'Massive hole!' I heard the driver tell Mr. Price. And so it was. For me, this was the first of its kind that I had seen. What must London look like? I thought. This after all was a single bomb, and some cities had hundreds dropped on them. As I scuffed my way back to the lorry through the descending night mist I thought again how I hated this war!

Guide night was the best one for me. I rushed my tea, changed into my uniform and was away. I recall that sometimes there was a certain bus which ran at irregular hours and sometimes not at all. One particular night I caught it going to town where I'd meet the others in the room at the Town Hall. It was good to be out and I could spend time on the bus thinking about this new poem my mind was dwelling on. The only other person on the bus was a soldier who was on a seat opposite me.

To help break up long hours on this dark, drab evening, the conductor began chatting to us both. I told him I was going to Guides and that I was an evacuee. 'From London?' he queried, and I tried to explain yes, but I had come from Cornwall to Wiltshire to my new school. At the mention of Cornwall the young soldier, and he seemed very young as he had a round baby face, shot over to the seat next to me. Before I knew it, he told me he came from Cornwall but not St. Ives, and he produced photos of his family. He was telling me who they all were, sisters and brothers, his Mum and Dad. He was animated, wanting to talk about them, but I'd arrived at my stop and had to get off. He looked near to tears and I saw how homesick he was, like that other soldier I had spoken to. Walking into the Town Hall I understood that they were both like me, far from home, loved ones and everything that was familiar.

At school, our art teacher Mr. Ames had us enthusiastic about painting country scenes. At first we drew from memory, something we had observed near where we lived, or on one of the nature rambles he or another teacher took us on. I enjoyed those classes, although not a very good artist. I liked doing the pencil drawings first and tried to draw some of the trees I had seen. At times we could, if we wished, draw different leaves from trees we had seen. It was winter now, so I drew some skeleton-like trees with my interpretation of a row of fields behind them. These fields I depicted as going into the distant skyline.

When I showed these to Mr. Ames, he asked, 'What did this scene make you think of Doris?'

'It looks like I feel,' I replied.

'And what's that?' he queried.

I had to think about this, then came up with, 'Sort of lost I guess, and the trees without their leaves look lonely.'

He told me it was a good picture. 'Perhaps one day you'll paint a picture like this.' He was reassuring, but I knew my art work wasn't that good, that I wouldn't paint a picture but might write a poem about it one day.

My Captain at Guides had asked if I would tell the troop how I helped to make fishing nets when I was in Cornwall, so the following week at the meeting I did. 'It's a bit like knitting,' I explained, 'but instead of knitting needles you use something called a shuttle, like you have on a sewing machine only much bigger.'

I remembered it all so clearly, making rows on the nets hanging on the Clares' door, and when they were finished taking them to be checked at the central place on the island in St. Ives. I wrote home and told Mum and Dad about doing the talk on Guide night, and also about my art work at school as I knew they'd be interested in that. I wondered if Dad was still able to draw now that his eyes were not good. He still worked and was an air-raid warden, he told me, and Mum passed on news about the neighbours I knew.

As well as writing to me they must have written to Mr. and Mrs. Price because Mum told me she would be coming to see me, just for a few days sometime nearer Spring. She must have been in touch with them, because Mrs. Price told me soon after that she would make arrangements for Mum to stay. When I heard from Mum again, she said she couldn't give a date yet as there were so many arrangements to make, but it wouldn't be too long before we saw each other again. I guess she had to make sure she wasn't working, that Dad could cope on his own, and sort out trains and the money.

I didn't dare to hope in case this wretched war intervened, so I just did things in the normal fashion, went to school and Guides, did my homework and waited. I think it was to be late March when Mum would arrive. Perhaps it was at Easter. It was decided by Mrs. Price that Celia would stay over with a friend or maybe a relative. That meant that I could have her bed in the room where she slept with Jane, and Mum would have my bed in my small room. I knew that in the end Celia had to stay with the relative, an aunt I think. I knew this because she was not very happy about it, and certainly she was not happy with me. Out of sight and hearing of her Mum and Dad she told me off, verbally and with a slight physical nudge or push if we passed each other in the house or outside. None of this mattered. I could ride it out and ignore it as Mum would be here soon.

It was not March when Mum came, or Easter. We had the school holidays for Easter in April and Mum was coming just after. She was to arrive on a Friday, but no one was sure of the time of her train, so I went to school just hoping the trains were running o.k.

Someone must have met her at the station, for when I got in from school there she was, and suddenly I was held by her and felt that rush of love I'd always known. Mrs. Price made her a cup of tea, and little Jane came and spoke to her.

She was only able to stay until Sunday and I wanted to tell her so much and have her all to myself, so when she had drunk her tea I took her out to show her the garden and the field beyond where the soldiers had camped one night. She told me how she and Dad were getting on. 'We've always got food because of the chickens and rabbits.'

As she told me this I remembered feeding the chickens we kept in the back garden, and the rabbit on top of the shed that I helped to look after. I told her how Mr. Price went ferreting and 'He skinned the rabbit he brought home, Mum, think he wanted to frighten me, but I didn't tell him I'd seen you do that and pluck the chickens when they'd been killed.'

With her arm round me we stood side by side with our backs to the Prices' home and gazed out through the railings onto the field. We didn't have to talk much, it was enough that we were together again. I didn't tell her that Celia bullied me a bit, and how sometimes I cried myself to sleep at night. I wouldn't let on because she and Dad were missing me so much. I knew that, and besides I was here in Trowbridge because it was safer.

I did tell her about the bomb that had dropped in a field though. 'We went to see the crater, Mum, such a big hole and only the one bomb! Everyone here thought it terrible.'

'Well they hadn't had it like London, so they thought it was bad,' she laughed, and hugged me tight; then we turned from looking through the railings and went back up the garden path and into the house.

After, I took Mum upstairs to show her my small room where she would sleep. She unpacked the few things she'd brought with her in a little case, things I remembered, the nightdress she had made, the hairbrush that usually sat on the mahogany dressing table in her and Dad's bedroom at home in Plaistow. She laid out the metal clippers that she used in her hair to make it a bit wavy. She'd put those in when she went to bed. Dad always used to laugh and say 'I just don't know how she sleeps in those.' Familiar patterns were all around me in that small room as she placed her things neatly on the little bedside table and the bed.

Downstairs again, Mr. Price was home and greeted Mum in his brusque way that I had become used to. Jane was in the kitchen helping her Mum, and I sat with mine whilst they were cooking the meal. It felt strange being in the room with Mum, it was awkward as no one spoke very much while the table was set and chairs pulled out. And after, when my Mum politely thanked them for the meal, there was still no conversation.

I suddenly realised that there never was a lot of conversation in that house, no sudden spurts of laughter, or general gossip about what had gone on during the day. Little Jane's voice was the lightest note as she spoke about her friends and the games they played.

The whole house seemed lacking in a kind of warmth between the family – not physical warmth in the house, that was o.k. I guess, but the comparison of what I had previously known, both in Plaistow with Mum and Dad and in St. Ives with the Clare family, was suddenly obvious to me. That sort of family connection, the vital quality, some underpinning of love was missing.

Looking across to where Mum sat in one of the straight backed wooden dining chairs, I wondered if she sensed it too, this lack of something that we'd always had in our home. I suppose I was coming to know the differences in other folk, in other areas and in other cultures. There was nothing wrong in how they lived their lives, I had just assumed that everyone and everywhere was the same. I had now discovered that there are certain differences which at that time seemed alien to me. I may well have understood if I had been a little older, but then it seemed as though I was living on a different planet.

It was an awkward time for Mum. She wanted to be, as always, just Mum, but this was not her home. She was a visitor but she must have felt like an intruder, while I felt the same, but not so much now an intruder, more an outsider and frightened that I would be thought of as a 'dirty Londoner'. Mum washed in the scullery like we all did, and she was 'Going to bed early,' she said, as she was tired after the journey. Although I was sleeping in Jane's bedroom, we didn't talk much. I just wanted the next day to arrive quickly and I would have Mum near me once more.

We went out soon after breakfast. Mr. Price went to work, and after I had cleared the dishes I took Mum into town and I pointed out the shops. I told her about the baker's and the lardy cake they made here, but not so much now because of short supplies of everything, flour, lard, dried fruit and sugar. 'When it's on sale, there are long queues,' I explained.

Mum laughed as she told me 'I know about queues!'

We went in the big main parish church, which I had never been inside. It had beautiful stained glass windows. She told me some of the stories they portrayed. After we came out we sat in the small green area near the Town Hall, so I was able to show her where I went to Guides. There were soldiers about in ones and twos, I guess on leave, and airmen too, who had some sort of insignia, Mum explained, to show they were Polish. She told me how they had lost their country and had come over to us to help fight against the nazis.

'How's Dad, and his eyes? Are they better?' I wanted to know.

'He will never have good sight, Dear.' I thought she had a sad look, then she brightened up. 'He is working at the moment and we get by.' She changed the conversation and warned me about speaking to any of the soldiers or other troops if I was out alone. So I thought it best not to tell her about the soldier on the bus as she might worry when she went home. At the thought of her returning I felt that thump again in my stomach which came with loneliness and homesickness. She had very little time with me, just another night and she would be gone.

In town we'd popped into Woolworths, where they had broken biscuits on sale. Mum bought some of these. She had selected a few of the better ones and they were put into loose bags. Back at the Prices', Celia had popped in for a while, so Mum gave the biscuits to her and Jane. 'Share them out later,' she told them, smiling.

We went to bed early again. We listened to the news on the wireless and then I went with Mum up to my bed with Jane. I kissed Mum goodnight at the top of the stairs, dreading tomorrow when she would go back to London.

Next morning I sat with Mum while we had toast and tea and, greatly honoured, Mum was given a boiled egg. 'As you have a long journey ahead,' Mrs. Price said rather sternly, as though the long journey was Mum's fault. Jane was out playing with her friends and Mr. Price was working in the garden, we were told.

Mrs. Price never spoke much to Mum, just imparted this sort of information. She never asked about how Mum and Dad had coped through the blitz, and Mum didn't enlighten her. And now, Mrs. Price was in a hurry to clear the table. Mum wanted to help her clear things but Mrs. Price said 'No, you best get your case and get to the station in case you miss your train.'

That thump was in my stomach again as I realised it was goodbye. 'I'll walk with you to the station, please Mum!' I was near to tears and Mum saw that.

'Best if we say goodbye here Dear,' she held me close. 'Seems a kind neighbour is walking with me to carry my case.' I stifled my tears and watched her go with Mr. Baker from along the road. Apparently arrangements had been made before she came, so I knew folk weren't unkind. Celia came back, and for once she was gentle with me. She could see how upset I was now Mum had gone. We went for a walk and ate the biscuits Mum had bought.

The days continued as ever, Springtime arrived, and the countryside seemed brighter. I was aware, deep inside me, that I would not be spending much longer in Wiltshire.

Chapter Seven - Decision

Echoes

Winter is losing its grip,
different air sidles in as frost deteriorates.
Snow no longer carpets gardens, pavements
and roads; little by little the signs appear,
as though past summers, lingering just out of sight
decide to tip new green above dank earth.

Regular as heartbeats old crocus buds appear,
and wild cyclamen emerge from undergrowth.

The north-east wind has stopped its spiteful bite.
Like smoky ash the clouds are hiding gold.
A pigeon struts complacently across the lawn
and hibernating tortoise creeps from sleep.

Soon trees, opening like fans, will spin
their shadows in the light, and birds will chorus
echoes of delight.

Soon we were in that delightful month of May. I felt brighter
and much happier. I enjoyed my time at school, with friends
there and after. There were two girls particularly that I became
friends with. We shared secrets, laughter and sometimes
sweets. Sweets were rationed but almost unobtainable, so
sometimes we'd try sucking certain cough drops which you
could still buy. We even tried doing the same with oxo cubes,

certainly an acquired taste!

Sweet rationing continued for many years, and the popular diary milk chocolate bar was withdrawn in 1941 as the government banned manufacturers from using fresh milk. A certain other chocolate bar was made. It was called ration chocolate and was made with skimmed milk powder; no silver paper round it, it was sold in a greaseproof wrapper. I remember the taste of this chocolate and found it horrid!

I liked the country better in the springtime, days were lighter and summer was on its way. Maybe the joy of seeing Mum during her short visit encouraged me to think ahead, to plan for the time when we'd be together again in Plaistow.

There was general talk at school about the summer holidays, and I heard some of the girls talking about going home for those weeks. It was made very clear by the headmaster at assembly one morning that it was necessary to sign a form if you were planning to do this. The form stated that you would be returning at the end of the school break. Suddenly my mind was made up. This was my opportunity and I didn't have to tell anyone, just go. I felt contained in a private little world, the one in my head that is. I wrote home and told them I had permission to come home for the summer, as we had been told that the bombing by the Luftwaffe was not so frequent now.

So one day, shortly after making my decision, I found myself in front of the headmaster's desk in the small room at school that he used as his office. I had been summoned there to sign the form as requested. He'd watched me carefully from his place behind that desk while I put my signature. Then abruptly he phrased a direct question. 'You will be returning, Doris?' I wondered if he asked everyone signing that form the same thing, or was it just me?

I had my hands behind my back and my index and middle fingers on both hands were crossed as I looked him straight in the eye and replied. 'Yes sir.' It was done.

Suddenly it was the school summer holidays and I was packing ready to leave. The Price family never said much, they only knew I had signed a form saying that I would be returning. I never told them that I was going to stay in London, I knew someone else would tell them.

The last night I said I'd be leaving with some of my friends. They would call together with two teachers who were also going home for the holidays. Mr. Price was not there when I left, Mrs. Price was busy as ever with sweeping and dusting and just wished me a good journey, and Celia did too. The only one I'd miss was little Jane, so I kissed her goodbye and gave her a copy of one of my small poems about Spring. I wonder if she still has it?

The school had made the travel arrangements from Trowbridge as a few of us were going home. Those others were excited, but I didn't feel like that until I was actually on the train taking me to London. My parents had been notified in good time for one or both of them to meet me. I confess I can't recall the main line station I arrived in, possibly Paddington.

This time someone would be there to meet me, and it was my mother. One look at the luggage I had brought with me and she said, 'You're not going back are you?'

On the way back to Plaistow by tube and other trains, I explained how unhappy I had been. 'I'm not going back.' She understood at once, and I told her 'I think Mr and Mrs Price knew I wouldn't be going back, although I never actually told them.' They must have known because I'd packed everything I possessed, including my precious books. My excitement had been contained all that previous week, even up to the time of my departure from Trowbridge. Sitting close beside my mother on the last part of the journey to Plaistow, I was tired and hungry but very happy. I knew I would never be going anywhere again as an evacuee.

During the time I'd been away I had received lots of letters from Mum and Dad. They told me that they were moving, not far from the flat we'd had. The reason was they had managed to buy a terraced house which they'd always wanted. So it was to this house I returned. I knew the area where it was so there was nothing strange for me to return to; it was still in Plaistow and I had a lovely bedroom all my own. The bed was a divan, and Mum explained how she planned to make a cover for it when she could get the material. It would have a frill all round the bottom of it, and I could choose which colour it would be in.

I picked up life again as I'd known it. Well not exactly, because all round me was evidence of what had been happening whilst I was away. Empty spaces where houses had been, others gutted or standing ruined with empty window frames and front doors blown off. One friend of ours who had lost his house took us to where it had stood. Only a few walls remained, but the front door was still in its frame with the door knocker on it! So for fun, we knocked on the door and walked into and round the empty frame. At least our friends had not lost their lives and one day they hoped to get another house.

Another building that had been bombed, well had a land mine dropped on it, was the school I should have returned to. It was a short walk from the new house we'd moved to, so we went to see the crater. No evidence of the school, just a huge hole in the ground. It had a high wire fence round it for the public's safety. As we stood gazing at this nothingness my Mum suddenly laughed and, turning to me, said, 'You know Doris, we were so pleased when we found we could move to our new house as it meant you wouldn't have far to go to school!'

Well it didn't mean that my schooling would stop. School authorities had dealt swiftly with this and other similar bombings of schools. Possibly either Dad or Mum contacted the Council, or maybe the Council and education authorities contacted them. Either way, when the autumn term began I had a bus ride to another Central School in Forest Gate. This was not a new building which my bombed out one had been. It was adequate enough, but had no grounds round it for games or gym, just a reasonably large concrete area.

Before term began my parents received a letter from the headmaster at the school I had left at Trowbridge. He informed her that she should realise what she was doing keeping me home as bombs were still falling, and he advised her to go and see a film the government had produced. This film described the outcome of bombings and what had happened during the worst of it. This to my parents who had been in London all through the blitz, while he had been in Wiltshire. My father, as usual, was calm about it, but my mother was irate and wanted to reply in detail and let this man know what she had been through. In the end she decided, or was persuaded by Dad I think, not to bother, and soon the matter was forgotten.

I was happy to go off to school, and this term of course I did have my school uniform. Although the gym slip was ok as Mum had allowed for my growth when she bought it, my arms, long and skinny, shot out from the cuffs of the shirts I wore. This was a big embarrassment for a young teenager.

We had proper classrooms with desks, not trestle tables, so I enjoyed the lessons more. We had a big hall for music and indoor games and gym. At dinner times when it rained, the upper forms were allowed to play dance records on a wind-up gramophone. Big bands, and jive and boogie woogie set that hall alight on those rainy days. Penny hops, we called them. There were lots of girls. Sometimes a few boys who were brave enough wandered in, and a few brave girls danced with them. Otherwise girls danced or jived together, and giggled and talked and enjoyed life.

I felt safe being home, safe within my known environment, not safe when the air raid warning sounded. We still had the bombing raids, although nothing like my parents had been through.

My part of Plaistow had certainly had its share of bombs. Other parts of West Ham had it considerably worse, Canning Town and the Tidal Basin area to name two. Nearer the docks, they had received day and night bombardments from the Luftwaffe. Houses, schools, shops were devastated. The Tidal Basin area, which Mum took me to see, was almost flattened. She told me how people had gone to shelter in a school which had also been hit by bombs, and many were killed and injured. As much as I'd hated being away from home, I was thankful that I had been, for a time, an evacuee.

When I'd first got back from Trowbridge Mum noticed that my teeth were not good. At that time you could receive treatment at the London Royal Dental hospital which was fairly easy for us to get to, and it was free. She took me several times and I had excellent treatment and was told I must clean my teeth regularly, which I confess I had not been doing whilst away from home.

The days she took me there she showed me other things. Mum was a country woman, but with Dad as her guide she had come to know London well. She showed me many fine buildings, and also the Nurse Edith Cavell memorial statue, and she told me the history of that brave lady who had helped so many during the first world war and been shot by the Germans for doing so.

One treat when we went to London was to go to Lyons Corner House for tea or lunch in the Brasserie there. There were several of these restaurants, and they remained open all through the war. They had underground shelters and some of their staff were trained as air raid wardens. Always busy, they opened early in the morning, and many who had spent their night in a public air raid shelter nearby would call in for breakfast on their way to work. Mum and Dad had sometimes spent evenings and nights in public shelters. 'This was during the worst of the blitz,' Mum told me. She went on to explain, 'We thought the brick built shelters might give us more safety.'

Then she laughed. 'Although of course, if they'd had a hit, bricks were a lot harder if they came on top of you than the Anderson shelter.'

I joined in her laughter, but couldn't imagine what it had been like for them. She continued telling me about those nights she and Dad had spent in the big public shelters. Once, an air raid warden came in with a lady he had found outside. She had been caught in a blast from a damaged building as it fell. 'Lucky to survive,' the warden told them, and went on to explain that she wasn't wounded, 'but has splinters in her eye which are painful.' He then asked if anyone in the shelter had some tweezers, as he could see the splinters and could remove them.

'What happened?' I asked eagerly.

'Well,' said Mum, 'of all the people in that shelter I was the only one who did have tweezers, as I always carry them with my nail file.'

'Was he able to remove the splinters?' I was eager to know how this story ended.

'Yes,' Mum continued. 'I handed them over and he was able to take the splinters out.' After she finished telling me this story she showed me the tweezers, which she still kept in her bag. They were to become mine and I still have them.

When we had tea or lunch in Lyons Corner House we often had to queue inside whilst waiting to be served. Even during the war it had an air of luxury about it, from the decor to the waitresses who were called nippies. They were all dressed the same with black dresses, starched white collars and aprons. and small white caps with a big red letter L embroidered on the front. It was a touch of glamour during those war filled days.

This touch of glamour made up for the times that we still had to dash to the Anderson shelter in the garden when the warning sounded. We had a little dog which barked when he heard that; he'd been with them through the blitz. Dad still did his turn as warden. They had buckets and stirrup pumps in case of fire. Skipper, our dog, didn't want to go down the shelter until we were all safely in. If Dad wasn't coming with us because he was on air raid warden duty he would stand at the top of the steps and bark continually. Dad waited to see all of us down those few wooden steps into the shelter, then picked up Skipper and quickly handed him to one of us.

'The raids aren't so close to us now,' Mum said, but we could hear the bumps and the loud 'crack, crack' of the anti aircraft guns as they fired at the enemy planes. These raids happened more often at night, so I did my school homework in that shelter. We had no proper light, only a small battery one which cast dim shadows. I used the lamp from my bike – also a battery one. Batteries were in short supply, so we tried to buy some whenever we could. We always kept candles handy, and matches.

If nights were cold Mum prepared cocoa in a large thermos and some food to take down the shelter if the siren went. If there was time after that dreaded sound she filled a hot water bottle to take with us. We had blankets and cushions always handy. Hopefully it wouldn't be a long time spent in the shelter as it was a bit cramped and cold down there. Whatever happened, I was home with those I loved.

Chapter Eight - Victory

OMAHA
(One of the D-Day Normandy Landing Beaches)

Where flatness of land extends to sea,
a man had no protection. His boots sank in soft sand,
and each slow movement between steps
filled him with terror.

In the noise of confusion he cradled his gun,
an alien weight, and responding
to shouted orders, he tried to run
interpreting forever the vastness of beach
as his own particular hell.

Now, out of season, the Normandy town
is empty, the seafront subdued and clean –
a solitary upturned boat a smudge on even sand.

The beach re-named Omaha
stretches interminably, bleached whiteness covering
old debris; water and salt have purified this place,
and a man returning, remembering,
walks on the sand welcoming the silence.

The days went by in the usual flurry of work for Mum and
Dad, although Mum had more days at home now. Dad's sight
grew progressively worse. On top of an accident he had
sustained many years previously, he had lost the sight
completely in one eye, and had glaucoma in the other with

nothing that could be done. The worry of it caused him to have severe stomach problems and he was in a great deal of pain at times, although he never complained.

During these bad times he had to lose days at work and had no pay coming in. Mum always found work for herself. Through all of this our home was bright and cheerful and full of love. The days Mum worked, a dear neighbour came in several times to check that Dad was fine, and she made him something to eat and cups of tea. Our little dog, Skipper, stayed close by his side. Dad liked the radio and he listened to it a great deal, and later when we were all home together, he would tell me about the music or the play he had listened to during the day. He knew certain poems and quotations and enjoyed saying them to me.

The war continued, days turned into months and the months into years. At school I was in classes for shorthand and typewriting. This was the reason my parents had, when filling in a form prior to my taking the eleven plus exam, selected Central School for me to attend. They could have put Grammar School, where some of my friends went. They explained to me that the Grammar meant you could sit for 'highers' or 'matric' as it was known. This, if passed, gave (hopeful) access to university. They had great faith that I would pass the eleven plus. However, as Dad patiently explained to me, 'We think it best if you go to the Central School where you will learn shorthand and typewriting, and one language.'

I knew what he meant. By learning these it meant I could probably get employment in an office in the city. 'And not,' as both he and Mum pointed out to me, 'have to work in a factory.' I understood. To them a job was necessary, but they didn't want me employed in one of the local factories, Jeyes Fluid, or Tate & Lyle the sugar company, to name a couple. There was nothing wrong with working in any of them; some of my friends were looking forward to doing just that. With my interest in books and literature, they hoped I would find a position where this could be put to good use.

Although food was in short supply we coped with rations. At times we still had occasional bombs dropped. Sometimes in the day at school, we had to leave our classrooms and hurry to a lower floor, where there were hardly any windows so not much glass that could be blasted in on us, and the walls were brick and sandbags had been piled outside to take any other blast.

I managed to pass typing exams, but what with the fear of air raids, and the fear of not having done my homework, I didn't sit the final shorthand one. I did get up to good speeds in both typing and shorthand which would be put on my leaving report. I also passed Grade 1 and 2 of the English R.S.A. Exams. There were no O or A levels then.

During those final years at school another weapon was launched at us from across the channel. These were the Vls and V2s and were very frightening. They were called by the letter V and considered by the Germans to be V for 'vergeltungswaffe' or revenge weapon. They started directing them at us soon after, and possibly in revenge for, the 6th June Normandy Landings, known as D Day landings.

The air raid warning sounded for the V1s. These were long range guided ballistic missiles. We heard them approaching, but it was when they cut out that it was so terrifying. We would count to eight, then wait for the sound of a thump and explosion, hoping it was far away from us. This went on, and we all coped as one had to. Because of the sound they made we called them buzz bombs or doodlebugs. This sound was like the noise of a two stroke motor cycle, then it would stop. It was like waiting for a silent bomb to drop from the sky. A worse V rocket was to come. This was called the V2 and there was no warning for this as it came so fast – and then the terrifying explosion where it landed.

I remember coming home from school one day, and once indoors, Mum told me, 'Come upstairs, I've had a lucky escape this afternoon.' If Mum was home from work she sometimes had a little nap in the afternoons, upstairs on her bed where she lay on top of the lovely blue eiderdown. No duvets then, just sheets, blanket and an eiderdown. This eiderdown was warm and cosy and full of feathers, supposedly from the eider duck. Mum entered her bedroom, closely followed by me. To my amazement the two sash windows in front of the bed and overlooking our street had lost most of their glass; and this glass was, to my shock, embedded in the eiderdown covering Mum and Dad's bed!

Mum laughed at my astonished look. 'It's all right,' she said. 'I'd had a bit of lunch and a cup of tea, so just stayed in my chair downstairs where I'd got comfortable.' She continued, 'Don't know where the blighter dropped, but he blasted our windows and along the street too.' I was just so thankful Mum hadn't been on that bed!

These doodlebugs, as we had come to call them, continued in a mini blitz of London. Since the Normandy Landings our troops and others were causing the Germans to retreat, and there was an upsurge of confidence in Britain that the war would soon end. However, the doodlebugs were demoralising and were continuing at a fast pace.

I had obtained a job in London, near Aldersgate Street, in an office, just as Dad had hoped. It was a publishing house. I would do a little typing, but mainly I was employed to read galley proofs, an essential job to closely read and edit work that was about to be published in dictionary form and encyclopaedias. Essential, but boring.

Nothing boring that first day I started there. On stepping out from the tube I found my way to the office which I had only attended once, on my interview for the job, and discovered it was barricaded. More than one doodlebug had been dropped there in the early hours. Buildings were shattered, debris and glass lay all around, water was spurting into the air from a burst water main. People hurrying to get to work brushed past me. I tried to go in the direction of my office, but a burly policeman and a fireman barred my way. I was so frightened that I would be late for my first job I didn't think about the dangers they were trying to keep me from. In the end the policeman showed me another way to get to the road where my office was. It was fine in the end. I made it by 9.a.m.

One morning at work an incident happened that will be forever fixed in my mind. About mid-morning the air raid warning went. There was no underground shelter, so people from my office, and several others from various companies who rented space in the same building, went to an oblong shaped room on the lower ground floor. I was at the far end and I couldn't see any of my working colleagues, but stood with others either side of me and along the two walls that led away from the door. There was no talking. A doodlebug was overhead, so we simply waited.

A young man who stood in the middle of about twenty other people suddenly walked over to where I stood. Much to my embarrassment he spreadeagled his body over mine. All of us waited, probably counting up to eight. I didn't hear the explosion, but a great release of tension was suddenly felt in the room and folk began to leave. It was then the young man across me walked back to the place where he had stood. I watched him light a cigarette and saw his hands were shaking. Glancing up, I realised why he had moved over to me and shielded my body. Directly opposite where I stood was a huge window almost floor to ceiling. If the missile had dropped on us, or nearby, the window might well have shattered and sent glass splinters and possibly the whole frame hurtling across the room into my body. That young man would have given his life for me. Strangely I never saw him again. He never worked in my office, and maybe he had to go into one of the armed forces after that incident. Wherever he was or is, I shall always be grateful.

At last I was able to spend Christmas in my proper home. I felt quite grown up now and I was earning money. I had taken R.S.A. English exams 1 and 2 grades at school and was tackling grade 3 at evening classes. I believe these are the equivalent of O levels nowadays. These, and certificates gained for both shorthand and typewriting, had helped me obtain the current job in London. If I passed the 3rd English exam I would look for a job that I hoped might be more interesting than reading galley proofs. I wrote poetry occasionally and thought I might be the future poet laureate!

When I left school my English teacher had given me a leaving present. This was her own copy of Virginibus Puerisque, by R.L. Stevenson. I considered this quite an honour, especially as she told me that it was her favourite book. Like other treasures, I still have this book.

At last the war was coming to an end. In 1944 the Royal Air Force were bombing the sites where the doodlebugs were launched from. The British Army and their allies advanced across France, Belgium and Holland, and they captured those dreadful launching sites. Finally, on the 8th May 1945, Germany surrendered. It was victory in Europe and proclaimed VE Day.

There was much celebration; street parties were held all over Britain and elsewhere. With some friends I went to the west end of London to join in with some of the happy crowd. We had fun, danced with strangers and laughed all through that night and into the early hours. We had to walk a fair way back to West Ham as it was the early hours of the morning before we started back and transport had ceased running. We were young and happy and utterly relieved to have no more bombings or doodlebugs falling. However, some were still waiting to celebrate, as the war in Asia had not ended. It was to be September that same year before Japan surrendered. This was victory over Japan and known as VJ Day.

What a great relief as men and women were demobbed

from the armed forces! Rationing was still in force and things of all description were still in short supply. I continued to work, but changed my job to an Importing/Exporting company near St.Paul's Cathedral. It was a better position, at first with a number of other typists, but then I was appointed secretary to one of the managers.

He was very interested to hear that I had been evacuated to live with someone who had worked in a factory on a wool carding machine. I told my new boss about the teasels that had been used when a machine broke down in the factory. He was interested in my story because he mainly imported and exported materials made from wool. I learnt from him about the warp and weft in material. I mainly typed shipping documents and his official letters to other companies.

It wasn't all work. I went out more, to theatres in London, to the cinema near Plaistow, and dances in Stratford which wasn't far from Plaistow. I was seventeen and had my share of friends, including boy friends – some of these from my school years. These boys were simply good friends. With them and some girl friends I would go swimming in the nearby baths as well as cycling together at weekends.

Then I met someone special. Some of the older pupils, men and women who had attended Russell Central school, decided now the war had ended to form an Old Students' Association. These past pupils of the school had just been demobbed from serving in the war, and having all met each other again, managed to book the hall in a local school each Friday evening for general activities. We had some music on a wind up gramophone, table tennis, plenty of chatter and much laughter, even a small drama group was formed. Simple enough fun by today's pleasures; but remember, we all in our different ways had been coping with the war years, and now we could enjoy our young lives and these Friday evenings were very good.

It was end of November 1945, and a bitterly cold

winter when a new group of young men, yes, men not boys, came along one Friday to the club. These had all been at school together and all of them had been in the war in various armed services. So at 18 years of age they had been conscripted and now at approximately 24 years old they were demobbed and ready to grasp at life again. They were so full of laughter enjoying each other's company, and watching them, I realised how good they must feel to have come through the war, and wondered what manner of things they had seen.

The second time they came, the snow had been falling for days and now, frozen over, it made for dangerous walking. As I walked across the playground to go home one Friday, chatting away to a group of my girl friends, I was suddenly hit in the eye by a snowball flung with considerable force by one of those young men. It was so forceful it knocked me off my feet and I lay flat on my back, while the one who had thrown it and one or two other bystanders laughed! I was highly indignant, although he helped me up and asked 'Let me take you for a drink.'

I was a bit haughty, I recollect. 'It's too late to go drinking!'

This man, whose name was Arthur, he told me, said, 'I've just been demobbed, I haven't got a whole lot of money on me, just thought I'd take you to the all night transport cafe for a cup of tea!' Who could resist? He had such an infectious smile and a twinkle in his eye, so I went. And that's how it all began.

That winter it remained cold. There was no central heating back then. Dad or Mum lit our fire, the only source of heating in our house, although we did have a paraffin stove, and a gas heater over the sink for hot water. Cold linoleum was on all the floors with a few rugs covering it, and carpet on the stairs. It was cold getting ready to go to work and I had bad chilblains on my feet, but I struggled as young women do to wear my smart shoes. We had rubber galoshes we wore over our shoes against the snow and sleet. Mum and Dad gave me some warm gloves, furry inside, for Christmas. Off I'd go to catch the train to London for work. It would be Christmas again soon, and just after I would be 18.

Mum's birthday was Christmas Eve and we always bought each other gifts for our birthdays, apart from Christmas presents. That first year home Mum had given me a lovely green glass powder bowl to have on my dressing table. I remember opening the carefully wrapped gift before leaving for work. I hugged Mum, and said 'It's so beautiful Mum, I'll keep it forever!' So far, I have kept my word.

During this cold time I still made it to Friday social club. Arthur was there. He rode in by bike. Even in the bitterest weather he came on his racing cycle, not in plus fours, though, which were sometimes worn by cyclists in extreme weather. He often wore shorts, but with warm tights underneath! Sounds strange? Yes, but that was usual, and worn by dedicated cyclists – which Arthur was. I found this out during the long conversations we had, at the youth club and also after when we went out together for meals, cinema, and dances.

He lived in Essex now, as on the first night of the blitz his mother and others were bombed out of their houses. They lived in Canning Town, slightly nearer to the docks than where I lived. He had been conscripted after both his brothers. The eldest had been called into the Royal Air Force, and his middle brother into the Army, and then Arthur into the Army. He'd been six years in the artillery, and now demobbed, he had found his old job had been given to the boss's son. This was not allowed, so this young man I hardly knew took his boss to court and won the day. 'It would have been very uncomfortable to have continued working for him though,' Arthur laughed as he told me how he'd handed in his notice as he left the court after winning his case. This, I decided, was a strong, brave, and very determined young man.

That December after Arthur and I had first met I

celebrated my 18th birthday. The bitter cold months continued. My Dad was progressively ill, on constant medication for his stomach problems and nearly blind. Today we know that glaucoma can be treated, but then it just seemed to get much worse. He had to give up work altogether and remained at home looked after by a neighbour, and Skipper who would not leave his side.

I met Arthur constantly, and also his family. His brothers had all returned safely from the war zones where they had been. His two sisters had to work in factories as part of their conscripted time. They all helped to support his mother who had been widowed when Arthur was only seven years old.

If I thought January was cold, February was worse. It was the coldest February on record. March came in just as cold. We had snow and then ice as it froze, food was still in short supply and so was fuel. Somehow we got through. Mum was working every day now to earn a little as Dad received no pension. My small amount each week helped, but they wouldn't accept it all as I bought my own clothes, etc. Dad kept the fire stoked and it was warm when we got home.

By the middle of March the thaw began. Ankle deep in slush I still managed to get out to meet Arthur, and by the following year we were engaged to be married. He had experienced more of war than I had, he had been in the D Day Landings and on the advance into Europe. He had then been sent to take part in the Middle East campaign that followed before coming home to be demobbed. My evacuee time was nothing in comparison with all that.

It would be several years later that we would return to Normandy and he could walk on those beaches, remembering, and think his own quiet thoughts.

In the spring and summer I joined the cycling club that Arthur belonged to, called The Becontree Wheelers. He was a racing cyclist, I discovered, and as these began again, he raced both on roads long distance, and grass tracks when available, as well as the concrete track at Herne Hill. He had a job now with the National Cyclist Union. In 1948 I was pleased to go to some of the cycling events that he organised for the Austerity Olympics, as they were called that year. He organised and helped at the two road cycling events held at Windsor Park, as well as the four track racing events held at the Herne Hill Velodrome. I was proud to see him wearing his official badge at these events.

I was prouder still in the following year, 1949, when my Dad, now almost blind, led me down the aisle in St.Mary's Church, Plaistow, where Arthur and I were married.

Epilogue

A decade, 1939 to 1949. So many years, so many memories. War time and peace time and in between. I have changed, as we all do. In fact this decade brought so many changes, indeed, the whole world changed.

Now a nonagenarian, I sometimes sit and watch my great grandchildren playing. At times when they roll a certain toy that rings a bell, I have an image flash through my mind of that long ago 'Muffin man', and me, buying muffins for tea.

L - #0137 - 011119 - C0 - 210/148/4 - PB - DID2663188